The Natural World

ASIA

Anita Yasuda

www.av2books.com

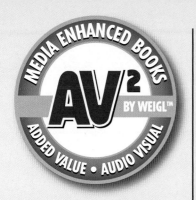

AV² provides enriched content that supplements and complements this book. Weigl's AV² books strive to create inspired learning and engage young minds in a total learning experience.

Your AV² Media Enhanced books come alive with...

Audio
Listen to sections of the book read aloud.

Key Words
Study vocabulary, and complete a matching word activity.

Video
Watch informative video clips.

Quizzes
Test your knowledge.

Embedded Weblinks
Gain additional information for research.

Slide Show
View images and captions, and prepare a presentation.

Try This!
Complete activities and hands-on experiments.

... and much, much more!

Go to **www.av2books.com,** and enter this book's unique code.

BOOK CODE

N 6 9 5 4 7 4

AV² by Weigl brings you media enhanced books that support active learning.

Published by AV² by Weigl
350 5th Avenue, 59th Floor
New York, NY 10118
Websites: www.av2books.com   www.weigl.com

Library of Congress Cataloging-in-Publication Data

Yasuda, Anita, author.
 Asia / Anita Yasuda.
     pages cm. -- (The natural world)
 Summary: "Land, oceans, and seas frame the Asian continent. The landscape of Asia ranges from deserts and tropical rain-forests to coral reefs and freshwater rivers. Learn more about this exciting environment in Asia. This is an AV2 media enhanced book. A unique book code printed on page 2 unlocks multimedia content. This book comes alive with video, audio, weblinks, slide shows, activities, hands-on experiments, and much more."-- Provided by publisher.
 Includes index.
 ISBN 978-1-4896-0942-7 (hardcover : alk. paper) -- ISBN 978-1-4896-0943-4 (softcover : alk. paper) --
ISBN 978-1-4896-0944-1 (single user ebk.) -- ISBN 978-1-4896-0945-8 (multi user ebk.)
 1. Natural history--Asia--Juvenile literature. 2. Ecology--Asia--Juvenile literature. 3. Asia--Environmental conditions--Juvenile literature. I. Title.
 QH179.Y37 2015
 578.095--dc23
                                    2014004671

Printed in the United States of America in North Mankato, Minnesota
1 2 3 4 5 6 7 8 9 0 18 17 16 15 14

042014
WEP150314

Project Coordinator: Heather Kissock
Design: Mandy Christiansen

Every reasonable effort has been made to trace ownership and to obtain permission to reprint copyright material. The publishers would be pleased to have any errors or omissions brought to their attention so that they may be corrected in subsequent printings.

Weigl acknowledges Getty Images as its primary image supplier for this title.

Contents

Welcome to Asia!

Asia is the largest of the world's seven continents. It has a land area that covers 17,226,200 square miles (44,614,000 square kilometers). This is roughly 30 percent of Earth's land mass. Asia's diverse **terrestrial** environments range from deserts to tropical rainforests. One of the most distinct physical features of Asia is the Himalayan Mountains, which cover 1,500 miles (2,400 km) and cut across India, Pakistan, Afghanistan, China, Bhutan, and Nepal. They include the tallest peak on Earth, Mount Everest.

Asia's rich plant and animal life are just part of what makes it a fascinating continent. People travel to Asia each year in hopes of seeing the giant panda, the Asian elephant, or Asia's rare trees, flowers, birds, and butterflies. Southeast Asia alone is home to one-fifth of all bird **species**.

A full-grown Asian elephant can eat up to 300 pounds (136 kg) of food per day.

At **40 inches** (1 m) across, the **Himalayan Rafflesia poppy** is the largest flower in the world.

Asia has 41% of the world's mangroves.

A giant panda eats 28 pounds (12.7 kg) of bamboo a day.

The giant panda lives in mountainous bamboo forests in parts of central China. These members of the bear family eat mostly bamboo.

Unique Asian Life

Asia has some of the most diverse species of plants and animals. Some plant and animal species are only found here. These are called endemic species. Two examples of endemic species found in Asia are the giant panda and the Javan rhinoceros. Endemic species are unique to a region. Some endemic Asian species are found throughout the continent, while others are confined to a small area. Rainforests on the islands of Borneo, Sumatra, and Java are home to many endemic species.

The jungles of Borneo are home to the proboscis monkey, known for its unusually long nose.

Borneo is the third-largest island in the world. Of the island's roughly 15,000 recorded plant species, 6,000 are unique to Borneo. The island is also home to 200 mammal species, including 44 endemics. A variety of reptiles and fish can be found on the island, as well as 1,400 species of amphibians.

A unique species of frog was recently discovered in Borneo. The frog does not have lungs. Instead, it absorbs oxygen through its skin. According to the World Wildlife Federation (WWF), three new species are discovered each month on Borneo.

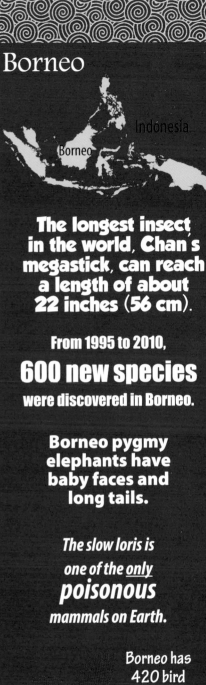

Borneo

Indonesia

Borneo

The longest insect in the world, Chan's megastick, can reach a length of about 22 inches (56 cm).

From 1995 to 2010,

600 new species

were discovered in Borneo.

Borneo pygmy elephants have baby faces and long tails.

The slow loris is one of the only
poisonous
mammals on Earth.

Borneo has 420 bird species. 37 of these species are endemic.

There are **12** species of flying squirrels. The pygmy flying squirrel is no bigger than a mouse!

Where in the World?

Land, oceans, and seas frame the Asian continent. An imaginary horizontal line called the equator splits the Earth into the northern and southern **hemispheres**. Most of the Asian continent is north of the equator. The countries here experience dry and cool climates compared to those that lie south of the equator. Countries near the equator are generally hot and humid throughout the year. Climate patterns affect the kinds of animals and plants that can live in a specific environment.

Southeast Asia has high humidity, temperate to tropical temperatures, and seasons of heavy rainfall called monsoons. Tropical rainforests thrive in this climate. Southeast Asia's rainforests have towering trees, thick vines, and rare plants. Some of these plants are highly valued for their use in medicines. Tigers, orangutans, hornbills, and fruit-eating bats are just a few of the animals found there.

Asian Biomes

Biomes are regions with the same climate and terrain. The living things found in a particular biome are **adapted** to survive the climate and geographic conditions of the area. Asia has several land biomes. These include grasslands, deserts, and a variety of forests. Grasslands can also be called steppes. Rainforests are near the equator. The deserts run across the continent to the Middle East. Taiga forests are in northern Asia.

The rainforests of Southeast Asia are the oldest in the world. Some date back 70 million years.

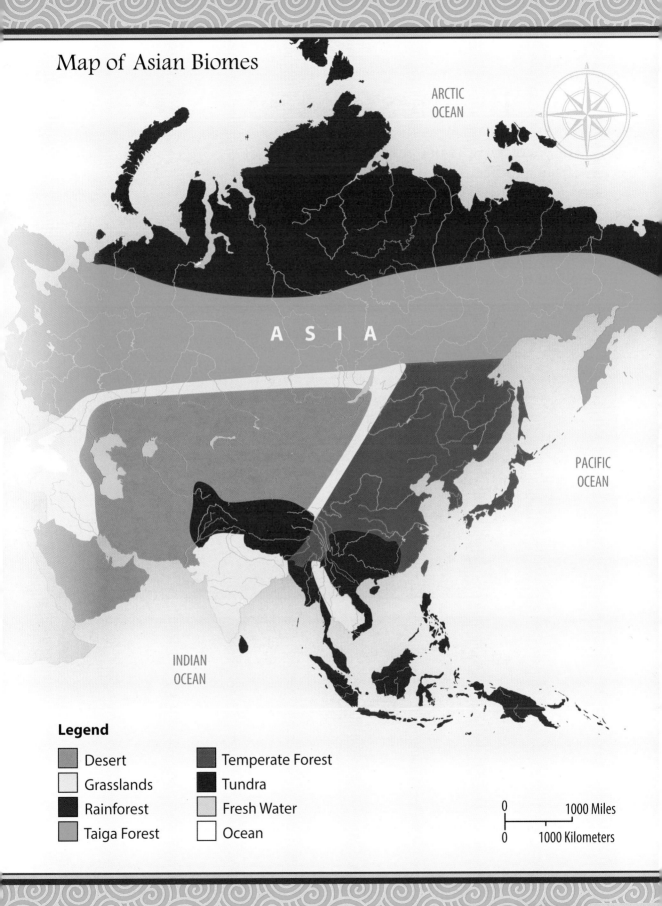

Map of Asian Biomes

ARCTIC
OCEAN

ASIA

PACIFIC
OCEAN

INDIAN
OCEAN

Legend

Desert		Temperate Forest	
Grasslands		Tundra	
Rainforest		Fresh Water	
Taiga Forest		Ocean	

0   1000 Miles
0   1000 Kilometers

Asian Land Biomes

The characteristics of one biome set it apart from another. Asia's principal biomes have characteristics they share with biomes on the other six continents. Plants and animals within a biome have adapted to its conditions. This is why plants and animals in similar biomes throughout the world have similar traits.

Grassland

These wide expanses of land are covered primarily in grass. The climate can be hot and dry.

Plants: Tufted grasses, wild tulips, irises, blue sage, camel's grass, and poppies grow throughout this biome.

Animals: Grazing animals, such as Bactrian camels and saiga antelope, rely on the biome's grasses. The sandgrouse, buzzard, and other birds feed on grass seeds, insects, and small animals.

Winter
44° to 59°F
(7° to 15°C)
Summer
77° to 109°F
(25° to 44°C)

Rainy Season
10 to 20″
(25 to 51 cm)

Taiga Forest

Taiga forests are thick groves of **conifers** such as pine, fir, and spruce. Summers are short, and winters are long.

Plants: This biome includes evergreen trees, mosses, lichens, and mushrooms.

Animals: Mammals living in the taiga include the ermine, lynx, and wolverine. Some birds, including the hawk owl, live here, too.

Winter
−65° to 30°F
(−54° to −1°C)
Summer
20° to 70°F
(−7° to 21°C)

Rainy Season
12 to 33″
(30 to 84 cm)

Even though these plants and animals share similar traits, they are not the same. Other factors in the environment, such as climate and terrain, will influence the way an animal or plant develops. Frogs are common in the hot, humid rainforests of Asia. However, a frog that lives in the rainforests of Sumatra may be different from a species that lives in the rainforests of Thailand.

Desert

Desert temperatures can fluctuate by 60°F (15.6°C) within a 24-hour period.

Plants: Shrubs and small trees store water in stems and deep roots. Hardy desert plants, such as acacia tree, tolerate high winds, sandstorms, and extreme temperatures.

Animals: Nocturnal animals escape the hot land surface by digging underground. Asian desert animals include the Arabian oryx, the long-eared jerboa, and Mongolian gazelle.

Summer
100° to 125°F
(38° to 52°C)
Winter
-40° to 0°F
(−40° to −18°C)

Rainy Season
4 to 6"
(10 to 15 cm)
per year

Rainforest

Rainforests have wet climates, warm temperatures, and moist air. Plants thrive in this humid climate.

Plants: Tall rainforest trees create a dense, leafy canopy. Shorter trees are found below the canopy. The forest floor is made up of mosses, grass, ferns, and flowering plants.

Animals: Animals live under the canopy because they find food, shelter, and water there. Asian rainforest animals include the Sumatran tiger, the sun bear, and the Asian elephant.

Average Temperature
80° to 95°F
(27° to 35°C)

Rainy Season
60 to 100"
(152 to 254 cm)

Asian Ecosystems and Habitats

An **ecosystem** includes land, air, water, and the populations of plant and animals that live there. Each living thing within an ecosystem has a specific role. Ecosystems consist of habitats. A habitat is the place where a species can find everything it needs to live, including food and shelter. Unlike an ecosystem, a habitat is specific to a population.

The Gobi Desert ecosystem in Mongolia and China is part of a desert biome. Bactrian camels, saiga antelope, and other hooved animals, such as the Siberian ibex, live in the desert and survive by eating the grasses, herbs, and shrubs found there. Snow leopards live in the mountains on the edges of the desert. The **endangered** Gobi bear lives there too and survives on wild onions, grass, berries, and sometimes, rodents.

The Toson Khulstai reserve, on the Mongolian Eastern Steppe, covers 1.2 million acres (4,856 sq. km). Temperatures here have been known to drop to as low as –50°F (–45°C). Few plant species can grow here, except shrubs.

The Gobi Desert has very little sand. Its primary features are its striking rock formations.

Taman Negara National Park is thought to be the oldest rainforest biome in the world. Parts of this rainforest may have been untouched since the ice age 130 million years ago. The forest is home to hundreds of bird species, which hide in the upper canopies and look for food in the thick undergrowth. One of the tallest plants in the forest is the massive 262-foot (80-m) tualang tree. The forest is also home to ferns, mosses, and orchids. Orangutans, monkeys, cats, and bears live here as well.

The color of the Siberian ibex enables it to blend into rocky surroundings. Males have the largest horns.

The eastern Siberian taiga has an area of 1,500,000 square miles (3,900,000 sq. km). This land is covered mostly with conifers, with some **deciduous** species such as birch. The taiga includes bogs, marshes, rivers, and lakes.

Plant Life in Asia

Asia's trees, grasses, and flowering plants have changed over thousands of years to survive the conditions of their habitats. Deserts are dotted with shrubs, small trees, and grasses that require very little water. Asian rainforests include a broad range of plants, from flowering and fruiting trees to ferns and vines. Rainforest trees include the fig, ginger, and acacia. The central Asian steppe may have up to 73 species of plants in a square yard (0.84 sq. m). The conifers of the taiga forests have also adapted to the conditions there. The shape of their needles helps them to absorb water.

Needlegrass is known by a few names. It can also be called feather grass and spear grass.

Needlegrass

Needlegrass belongs to the stipa family. The grass matures in the spring and has long green leaves, and narrow stems. This grass grows about 3 feet (91 cm) high. It can survive through dry conditions, intense sunlight, and high winds.

Pitcher Plants

Borneo has more than 36 species of pitcher plants. These plants thrive in the moist and warm conditions. Pitcher plants are **carnivorous** and use color, taste, and smell to lure their prey. The slippery rim of the pitcher plant makes it easy for unsuspecting insects to fall into the pitcher. Scientists discovered that rainforest bats use these plants for shelter. Bat droppings provide nutrients for the plants.

The pitcher plant is one of the few carnivorous plants in the world.

Scots Pine

The Scots pine is commonly found in the frozen taiga forests of northern Asia. There, the growing season is short, and the soil is acidic. The towering, narrow shape of this tree allows it to shed snow from its branches, which prevents them from snapping off.

The Scots pine is the one of the world's most widespread conifers. Its native range stretches from the Arctic to Asia's central deserts.

Juniper Tree

The juniper tree thrives in the dry, sandy, and rocky soil of deserts. In Asia, junipers are found from China to Saudi Arabia. Birds and other desert animals, including mammals, flock to the juniper for its berries and seeds.

Juniper trees can grow at altitudes up to 13,000 feet (4,000 m).

Just the Facts

The rafflesia, from Malaysia, is the heaviest flower in the world. It can weigh more than 22 pounds (11 kg).

More than 10,000 plant species grow in the tropical rainforests of Sumatra.

The saxaul tree collects water behind its bark. People in the desert can squeeze it for a drink.

A tualang tree can be home to up to 30,000 bees.

The metasequoia is believed to be one of the oldest and rarest trees in the world.

Insects, Reptiles, and Amphibians

Dragonflies, stick insects, crickets, and butterflies are some of the hundreds of thousands of insects in Asia. Some, such as the Asian giant hornet, are dangerous, and others, such as the camel spider, are fast. Camel spiders can run up to 10 miles (16 km) per hour.

There are a wide variety of reptiles and amphibians in Asia, from tiny frogs to salamanders that weigh 55 pounds (25 kg). The reticulated python is a very large snake, at 33 feet (10 m) in length. The world's smallest vertebrate, a frog measuring only 0.3 inches (0.8 cm), also lives in Asia. Reptiles and amphibians commonly eat insects.

The giant spiny stick insect is a nocturnal animal. It hides under bark and in tree hollows during the day.

Giant Spiny Stick Insect

The giant spiny stick insect looks like a walking piece of bark or leaf. Generally, it is found on the lower half of a tree trunk or on the ground. It is hard for predators to find the insect because it successfully blends into the foliage.

Rumanzovia Swallowtail

This striking butterfly is found in Southeast Asia and Australia. Males have black forewings with white edges and red spots on their black hind wings. Females come in a variety of color combinations, including black with red spots. A Rumanzovia swallowtail's wings can span up to 5 inches (12.7 cm).

The Rumanzovia female lays eggs on the leaves of citrus trees. The leaves act as a food source for the hatched larvae.

Komodo Dragon

Found on only five Indonesian islands, the Komodo dragon is the largest lizard in the world. It has a life span of roughly 30 years. Males can grow to 10 feet (3 m) in length. Females are smaller. The Komodo dragon uses its sharp claws and teeth to kill prey such as wild pigs and goats.

The Komodo dragon is the dominant predator of its ecosystem. It feeds on mammals as large as deer and water buffalo.

Long-nosed Horned Frog

This frog is commonly found in the rainforest underbrush of Southeast Asia, including Malaysia and Thailand. Its skin color looks like leaves. This coloring hides the frog from predators and allows it to sneak up on prey.

The long-nosed horned frog is named for its elongated snout and upper eyelids, which extend to look like horns.

Just the Facts

The Bengal monitor lizard eats more than 200 types of prey, including smaller reptiles, birds, and birds' eggs.

A Komodo dragon can weigh more than *300* pounds (136 kg).

Asians believe that the cricket is a symbol of good luck.

The Chinese bird spider has a leg span of 8 inches (20 cm).

The Asian paradise tree snake can glide as far as 300 feet (91 m) through the air by flattening its body to almost twice its width.

The Burmese python, at 25 feet (7.6 m) in length, is the third largest type of snake in the world.

Birds and Mammals

Three Asian countries are among the top ten for mammal diversity. Indonesia has the most mammal species in the world, with 670. China and India follow, with 551, and 412 respectively. Many of these mammals are **ungulates**. These include the Bactrian camel, black rhinoceros, and water buffalo. Asia also has 79 primate species. One of the rarest and most endangered primates is the Sumatran orangutan, which lives in the rainforests of Sumatra. Some rare carnivores live in Asia as well. These meat-eaters, such as the clouded leopard, feed on deer, monkeys, pigs, and smaller animals such as squirrels. Asia also has more than 3,000 species of birds.

Leopards are the smallest of the big cats. They are, however, the most widespread, with populations in both Asia and Africa.

Leopard

The leopard is found throughout Asia's rainforests. It can grow from 3 to 6.2 feet (91 to 189 cm) long and run up to 36 miles (58 km) per hour to capture prey. The leopard generally sleeps during the day and hunts at night when it is cooler. It eats different types of prey, including monkeys, amphibians, large birds, and fish.

Bali Mynah

The northwestern tip of Bali is home to this stunning bird. The Bali mynah makes its home in trees or cliffs, where it feeds on seeds, worms, and insects. Mynahs are currently on the endangered species list because their habitat is being destroyed by logging. The mynah is also the target of the illegal pet trade.

Scientists estimate that there are only about 115 Bali mynahs living in nature.

Takin

The takin belongs to the antelope family. It lives in small herds in the taiga forests of China and the Himalayas. Takins have strong legs and solid hoofs, which help them navigate the rough terrain. The takin ranges in height from about 3 to 4.5 feet (0.9 to 1.4 m), and can weigh up to 770 pounds (349 kg). A takin eats a wide range of vegetation, including evergreens, bamboo leaves, and pine bark. The animal pushes over small trees with its body to reach the top leaves.

Takins migrate up the mountains in the spring and then move to the lower valleys during the fall.

Przewalski's Horse

Przewalski's horse lives in the steppes, grassy deserts, and plains in China, Mongolia, and Kazakhstan. The climate of northern Asia is cold. The horse survives because it has a thick coat that keeps it warm in the winter months. In 1970, Przewalski's horse was declared extinct because it only existed in zoos. In recent years, it has been reintroduced to its natural habitat.

More than 300 Przewalski's horses have been reintroduced to their natural habitat since 1992.

Just the Facts

Bamboo leaves are 90% of the red panda's diet.

By drinking dew from trees, the Arabian oryx can go without water for weeks.

The orangutan is the only great ape found on the Asian continent.

A leopard can climb a 50-foot (15-m) tree carrying prey that is larger than itself.

Asian elephants can grow up to 21 feet (6.4 m) long and stand up to 10 feet (3 m) tall.

Asian Aquatic Biomes

Asia has two main aquatic biomes. These biomes are classified as either freshwater or marine. The main factor separating these biomes is the salt content in the water. In addition to aquatic plants, animals such as waterfowl, fish, amphibians, and some mammals live in water environments.

Aquatic Ecosystems and Habitats

Three percent of Earth's water is fresh water. Fresh water can be found in icecaps, streams, lakes, and rivers. The largest freshwater lake in Asia is Russia's Lake Baikal. It is estimated to hold one fifth of the world's fresh water. China's Yangtze River is the longest river in Asia. It measures 3,915 miles (6,300 km) in length and flows eastward to the East China Sea.

Freshwater Biome

Freshwater biomes include coastal regions and wetlands, such as marshes, mudflats, and **peatlands**. The flow rate and amount of water in Asian streams and rivers determine the organisms that live in these ecosystems.

Plants: Algae, reeds, grasses, and water lilies are just some of the aquatic plants found in Asia's freshwater biome.

Less than 1% salt content

Animals: Mammals, birds, fish, reptiles, and amphibians all rely on the watery environment of the wetlands. Animals living here include sturgeon, plankton, turtles, crocodiles, otters, and waterfowl.

The marine biomes are known for their large expanses of ocean and coral reefs. These areas are home to many creatures, ranging from tiny reef-building plants to huge mammals. Asia's coral reefs are found along the southern coasts of the continent. Indonesia has the most coral reefs in the world. These reefs have more than three-quarters of the world's known coral species. However, many species of plants, fish, crabs, shrimps, mollusks, turtles, and sharks also live in and around the reefs.

Mangroves can also be found in the marine biome. These forests grow in swampy areas that are partly on land and partly in water.

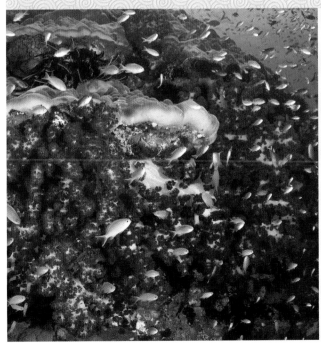

Marine Biome

The seabed, mangroves, coral reefs, and the Pacific, Arctic, and Indian Oceans make up Asia's marine biome. Three-quarters of all marine life live near the surface of the water, where they receive the greatest amount of light and warmth from the Sun.

Plants: The marine biome hosts a variety of aquatic plants, including algae, kelp, seaweed, seagrass, and **diatoms.**

About 3% salt content

Animals: Sea turtles, fish, sharks, stingrays, whales, seals, otters, dolphins, jellyfish, and squid can all be found in the waters of Asia's marine biome.

Asian Aquatic Life

The types of plants and animals that live in a freshwater or marine biome depend on certain conditions, including water depth, temperature, nutrients, and amount of light available. Algae make up a large part of aquatic life and have adapted to live in either freshwater or saltwater biomes. Fish species are also divided into freshwater or saltwater varieties. Many bird species, including the white ibis, live in saltwater habitats. Other birds, such as the Siberian crane, prefer freshwater lakes. Freshwater habitats also attract large mammals.

Water Buffalo

The water buffalo is an impressive 5 to 6.2 feet (1.5 to 1.9 m) in height. These large mammals typically weigh between 1,500 and 2,600 pounds (680 to 1,179 kg). They are most often found sitting in the muddy waters of wetlands and swamps of Asia. Mud helps keep this mammal cool and protects it from biting insects. Water buffalo eat aquatic plants, grass, and herbs.

Water buffalo often use their horns to scoop mud onto their backs. This helps keep insects away.

Red-crowned Crane

The red-crowned crane is considered an endangered species. There are less than 2,000 in the wild. The red-crowned crane feeds in the deep-water marshes, where it finds many types of insects, fish, amphibians, snails, and mollusks to eat. The red-crowned crane is the national bird of Japan and is considered a symbol of good luck in China.

Red-crowned cranes are known for their elaborate courtship rituals. Breeding pairs mate for life.

Hawksbill Turtle

The hawksbill turtle lives in many of the world's oceans. In Asia, it is found in the Pacific and Indian Oceans. This turtle prefers the coastline, shallow lagoons, and coral reefs to the open sea. Here, its main food source, the sea sponge, is plentiful. The hawksbill turtle is omnivorous. This means it eats both plants and animals. Mollusks, sea urchins, and jellyfish make up part of its diet.

The hawksbill turtle gets its name from its beak-like mouth.

Chinese River Dolphin

The Chinese river dolphin is one of the rarest species of dolphin. It lives in the Yangtze River. In 2006, scientists declared this dolphin extinct, but in 2007 they changed the status to critically endangered when one was found swimming in the Yangtze River. This dolphin weighed about 500 pounds (227 kg) and was 8 feet (2.4 m) in length. It was gray, with lighter gray on its belly, and it had a long beak.

The Chinese river dolphin is one of only four freshwater dolphin species alive today.

Just the Facts

Even though the Caspian Sea is inland, it is the largest saltwater lake in the world.

Out of the world's 7 marine turtle species, 6 live in the Asia-Pacific region.

The Mekong giant catfish is the largest freshwater fish in the world. It grows to 10 feet (3 m) long and can weigh up to 650 pounds (294 kg).

The largest Asian coral reef is 50 miles (80 km) in length.

Asia has 42% of the world's mangroves.

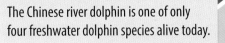

Maintaining Balance

A healthy, functioning ecosystem needs to be in balance. Changes to an ecosystem can affect the species that live there. A severe drought or extreme cold can damage the plant life that some animals depend on for food. There are also other ways an ecosystem can be out of balance.

Introducing New Species

If a new, non-native species is introduced to an ecosystem, the ecosystem becomes unbalanced. The new species will compete with native species for food, shelter, air, and water. The population of the new species can increase very quickly if it has no natural predators in the area. If the new population grows unchecked, it may start to overtake the ecosystem. Eventually, native species may die off from a lack of resources, or the native population will move to another area.

One report estimates that nearly all fresh waterways in Southeast Asia have been invaded by non-native plant species. These invaders include water lettuce, water hyacinth, and yellow burhead. These plants grow on the surface of waterways such as lakes, making it difficult for boats to pass through. They reduce the oxygen levels in water, which causes other living things to die. Removing these invading species is costly. Not all invaders are plants. Some lakes have been overtaken by non-native fish, such as tilapia. In the Philippines, non-native fish have caused the extinction of endemic lake fish.

Water hyacinths clog many of the waterways of Southeast Asia.

Ecosystem Interactions

The interactions of organisms can be represented by a food chain. Every food chain contains producers, consumers, and decomposers. Plants are producers because they use the Sun's energy to make food. Primary consumers are herbivores that eat mainly plants. Secondary consumers are carnivores and omnivores, which feed on the herbivores. Decomposers include the insects or fungi that recycle decaying matter.

Tapirs

Tapirs are primary consumers in the southern rainforest. These herbivores feed on flowers, leaves, nectar, and fallen fruits. The tapir helps spread seeds when those seeds pass through its digestive system. Tapirs are hunted by large cats such as leopards and tigers.

Ferns and Damar Trees

Ferns and damar trees are producers. Ferns and fruit from the damar tree provide food for animals such as orangutans, macaques, squirrels, and rhinoceros hornbills.

Sumatran Tiger

Sumatran tigers are secondary consumers that feed on tapirs and other animals, including sambar deer, jackals, and wild pigs. They blend into the thick underbrush of the rainforest and lie in wait for prey.

Pangolins

Pangolins use their sharp claws to tear into termite mounds and ant nests. They use their sticky tongues to catch the ants and termites. Carnivores such as tigers prey upon pangolins.

Termites and Ants

These insects eat organic matter, including ferns and fruit from the damar tree, competing for food with animals like the tapir.

Diversity for Humans

Asia's diversity of plant and animal life has provided important resources for its people for thousands of years. Asia includes six of the top 10 fish-producing countries in the world. In addition, Asia is one of the most important sources of many food crops. Bananas, mangos, plantains, citrus fruits, and spices such as cardamom, ginger, and tea grow there.

Human Impact

Human activity is threatening the habitats of the plants and animals of Asia. According to the WWF, humans pose the largest threat to species survival. People are clearing trees and other plants in these habitats to satisfy the demand for land for development or agricultural use. Often, when land is cleared, the crops that are planted in place of native species are not suited to the land.

It is estimated that only 2 percent of China's native forests remain intact. Many of these forests are cut down to make room for non-native trees. Eucalyptus trees, for instance, are grown to improve pulp and paper production in the country.

Reduction in habitat size can lead to overcrowding. The area cannot always support all of the organisms living there. Competition for food increases. If animals can no longer find food, they must leave the area or starve. In Sumatra, conflicts between farmers and orangutans or macaques have increased because these animals are forced to raid farmers fields for food.

Indonesia has one of the most threatened rainforests in the world. The forest is being cut down so that palm oil plantations can expand. When a habitat is destroyed, a species is deprived of its food, water, and protection. The population becomes vulnerable to extinction.

An orangutan depends heavily on the forest for its survival. Its habitat is shrinking as humans develop forest land.

Conserving Nature

Development in or near fragile habitats must be **sustainable**. Governments and private organizations are encouraging scientists and scholars to come up with plans to maintain habitats, reintroduce species, and even discover new ones.

Asia has more than 4,000 terrestrial and marine protected areas. Some are **ecological reserves** and national parks, which are destinations for **ecotourism**. Ecotourism encourages tourists to visit natural areas with the hope that it will raise awareness. The money generated benefits conservation and research.

Leopards are critically endangered and will become extinct without conservation measures.

Make an Ecosystem Web

Use this book, and research on the internet, to create an Asian ecosystem.

1. Choose an Asian plant or animal. Think about its habitat.
2. Find at least three organisms that live in the same habitat. This could include plants, insects, amphibians, reptiles, birds, and mammals.
3. How do these species interact with each other? Do they provide food or shelter for the other organisms?
4. Link these organisms together to show which rely on each other for food or shelter.
5. Once your ecosystem web is complete, think about how removing one organism would affect the other organisms in the web.

Asian Ecosystem

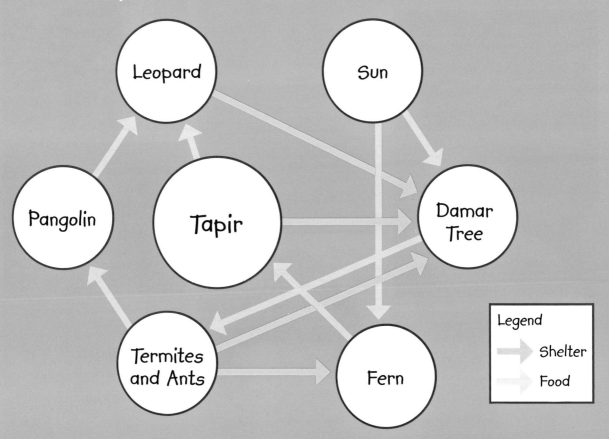

Quiz

2 What is a species that is unique to a region called?

Endemic

3 What are the seasons of heavy rainfall called?

Monsoons

1 Which region of Asia includes the taiga biome?

Northern Asia

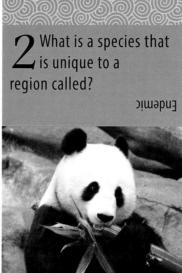

6 Name three non-native plant species that have invaded Southeast Asia.

Water lettuce, water hyacinth, and yellow burhead

5 How many endemic plant species are found on Borneo?

6,000

4 What is a habitat?

A place where a species has everything it needs to live

7 Where does the Komodo dragon live in nature?

Indonesia

8 What is the most endangered primate in the Sumatran rainforest?

Orangutan

9 Name the two main types of aquatic biomes?

Freshwater and marine

10 What is destroying the Bali mynah's home?

Logging

Key Words

adapted: changed to suit an environment

carnivorous: feeding on other animals

conifers: evergreen trees with needle-shaped leaves

deciduous: trees and bushes that lose their leaves in the fall

diatoms: microscopic water plants

ecological reserves: regions with protected plants and animals

ecosystem: a community of living things sharing an environment

ecotourism: the business of touring natural environments to conserve them

endangered: a species that is in danger of dying out

hemispheres: equally divided halves of a sphere

nocturnal: animals that are active at night

peatlands: wetlands with layers of decaying plants

species: a group of animals or plants that share similar features

sustainable: using resources so they are available for future generations

terrestrial: land-based

ungulates: animals with hooves

Index

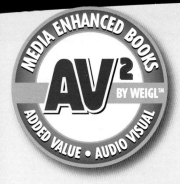

Log on to www.av2books.com

AV² by Weigl brings you media enhanced books that support active learning. Go to www.av2books.com, and enter the special code found on page 2 of this book. You will gain access to enriched and enhanced content that supplements and complements this book. Content includes video, audio, weblinks, quizzes, a slide show, and activities.

AV² Online Navigation

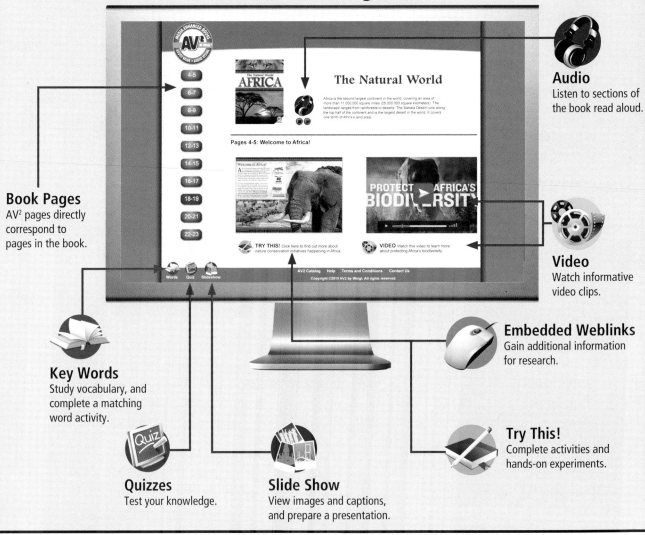

Audio
Listen to sections of the book read aloud.

Video
Watch informative video clips.

Embedded Weblinks
Gain additional information for research.

Try This!
Complete activities and hands-on experiments.

Book Pages
AV² pages directly correspond to pages in the book.

Key Words
Study vocabulary, and complete a matching word activity.

Quizzes
Test your knowledge.

Slide Show
View images and captions, and prepare a presentation.

AV² was built to bridge the gap between print and digital. We encourage you to tell us what you like and what you want to see in the future.

Sign up to be an AV² Ambassador at www.av2books.com/ambassador.